INTRODUCTION

Friendly Street's New Poets series publishes poets whose work has not previously appeared in collection form.

In a sense, the term 'New Poets' is misleading. The three poets in this compilation are poets who have been refining their craft for years. Their very individual poetic voices – reflective, engaging and observant – are imbued with experience.

Though these voices are familiar to Friendly Street audiences, it is timely that, with the publication of this book, they speak to a wider audience. It is my privilege to invite you to be part of that audience, to enter into the atmospheres, images and musings that await you in the following pages. Please accept the invitation!

David Adès,
Convenor
Friendly Street Poets

FRIENDLY STREET

new poets eight

The Windmill's Song Elaine Barker

Kite Lady Tess Driver

Fine Rain Straight Down David Mortimer

Friendly Street Poets

Wakefield Press

Friendly Street Poets Incorporated
in association with
Wakefield Press
Box 2266
Kent Town
South Australia 5071

www.friendlystreetpoets.org.au
www.wakefieldpress.com.au

First Published 2003

Cover illustration by Jonathon Inverarity
Designed by Gina Inverarity
Typeset by Clinton Ellicott
Printed and bound by Hyde Park Press, Adelaide

ISBN 1 86254 608 8

  Friendly Street is supported by the
South Australian Government
through Arts SA.

Government
of South Australia   A R T S A

 Wakefield Press thanks Fox Creek Wines
Fox Creek   and Arts South Australia for their support.
Wines

CONTENTS

THE WINDMILL'S SONG
Elaine Barker
1

KITE LADY
Tess Driver
31

FINE RAIN STRAIGHT DOWN
David Mortimer
61

THE WINDMILL'S SONG

Poems of the Riverland

by Elaine Barker

Elaine Barker spent her childhood in the Riverland. Formerly a librarian, she graduated from the University of Adelaide as a mature age student with an M.A. in English Literature. She has run courses in Creative Writing for many years and reads regularly at Friendly Street. This is her first collection of poetry.

ACKNOWLEDGEMENTS

Friendly Street Reader 22 for 'The Schoolbook
Left Behind', *Friendly Street Reader 23* for
'Processionary Caterpillars', *Canberra Times*
for 'Molly', *New England Review* for 'Summer
Secrets', *Sydney Morning Herald* for 'Seascape',
Friendly Street Reader 21 for 'Old Plough',
Bulletin and *Friendly Street Reader 15* for
'In Grandmother's Garden', *Friendly Street
Reader 26* for 'Tribute', *Blue Dog* for
'At Donovans' Milkbar', *Canberra Times* for
'Sanctuary', *Bunyip* for 'On The River,
Late Summer', *Friendly Street Reader 24* for
'On the River' (Satura Prize, 2000).

With special thanks to Yve Louis.

For the late Denis
and for
Tony, Victoria and Juliet

THE POEMS

Harvest 4

Travelling back 6

The Schoolbook Left Behind 7

Processionary Caterpillars 8

Skyline 9

In our backyard a figtree 10

Skipping Song For Katherine Clive 11

Manoeuvres 12

Kiss It Better 13

Molly 14

Nightwatch 15

Summer Secrets 16

Seascape 17

Recollection 18

Old Plough 19

Compensation 20

In Grandmother's Garden 21

Tribute 22

At Donovans' Milkbar 23

After the Dance 24

Sanctuary 25

On The River, Late Summer 26

River Red Gum 27

On the River 28

Harvest

The way of the river, strung along
irrigation channels to reach
well beyond the town, released
in double furrows, sunstruck,
between rows of apricot, peach,
orange, thick-foliaged vine.
There amongst the vines we raced
and splashed free as we cared to be,
trying to hold the hurry of water,
forming castles, ditches, walls, dams.
The way we patted neat mud pies,
went mad with mud, with wet red earth.
The way we chucked it all around.
We even pelted little sparrows.
But, knowingly, made good the furrows
before leafy passageways took us in,
where suckling like young animals
we pulled at the fruit until our arms,
faces, were awash with grape juices.
At rest in this bluegreen shadowline
rippled with light we'd hear
above the nearby windmill's murmur,
the close familiar teasing gurgle
lapping in front of us and behind.
How those twin rivers raced me down
a radiant pathway that unravelled
far-off, fading into a blur.

Around me a mystery – the way
the sun spun and caught sparkles
from the holiday song of water
under the flight of the sky.
That sound was like laughter.
There was a rightness though, and order.

Travelling back

through my childhood I follow a road
that shimmers in summer beyond the town.
I take the path that hugs the road
from home to school then back again.
There was a tune I knew –
at Easter time the lilies fair
and lovely flowers bloom everywhere.
But here only wattle, ti-trees,
some scrubby gums, though a place
spiced with yellow-tipped mustard weed.
And a scatter of burrows.
You could spot a rabbit now,
even by day. My track straggles
over sand drifts where roly-polies
drawn against barbed wire fences
lock into taut disorder along the way.
The soil loosens, shifts,
slips in to half-fill your sandals
as you journey on so always you take
a portion of that path with you,
its grit, the weight of its warmth.

The Schoolbook Left Behind

I remember my father,
the shout of his arm.
His steps raised trumpets of dust
from the earth as he ran,
his head thrown forward,
shirt a khaki brown.
I had stopped my bicycle,
stood waiting near a ti-tree
in the slack Mallee sand.

Today his words are forgotten
and the book he brought me
has faded to sepia
at the back of my mind.
But I still picture my father
as he made his way home
and that walk he had
and the sulking of crows,
the stubble field around.

Processionary Caterpillars

You know the way you used to find
those caterpillars in one dark line,
a softly undulating furry chain,
a strangely straight and murky rainbow
with no known beginning and no end.
One day when I was nine
I stamped on a rippling velvet trail
like that, then stepped aside to watch
the frothing crumpled writhing mess,
green ooze sliming the ground.
Appalled at what I'd done
I turned, ran. I looked back once
and saw the creatures joined again
in orderly procession,
end to end in a vibrant line –
a gash across the land.

Skyline

Early morning sees blueshadowed clouds flow,
spill out beyond their boundaries
reforming monumentally as they sweep along.
With its yellow message my boxkite soars
there too and tugs against the void.
Light sheens a crow that idles,
slides away then rises like a tick
for good work on a schoolbook sky.

Down here closepruned peachtrees
turn to stickmen as they march by.
Our track is still fastfrosted,
the stunted bushes catherinewheels
spinning cobwebs and diamonds
over the undergrowth on either side.

A winter morning with my kite
flying from a splintered post
and barbed wire fence nearby,
my white hand in command
of the rippling line, my kite
cloudreaching, skylarking with crows.

In our backyard a figtree

large enough to form a house.
Hours on end we fought or played there,
each room contained, marked out
with stones. Neat lines of ants
shifting daily, up to something,
would map their own domains
or make for the kitchen where chairs
and a table offered biscuit crumbs.
Come, you'll see boxes loud with comics,
my doll Patsy framed by her pram,
a sunny place where the dog creeps in.
I remember this: in the bathroom
a bottle filled with yellow piss.
Branches shaped the upper floor
from where we cut a window, took in
the windmill, the way it groaned,
it turned, it fractured light.
And all around, the pulsing rasp
of the windmill's song. Outside
leafy walls fell clear to the ground.
The figs suspended there were rich
and dark as children's sorrows
and just as hidden, forever at hand.

Skipping Song For Katherine Clive

One two three four five
our little Katie went home alive
six seven eight nine ten
didn't come back to school again
one two three four five
soon the coppers began to arrive
six seven eight nine ten
all of them went hunting then
one two three four five
went out looking for Katie Clive
six seven eight nine ten
found her with her knickers down
one two three four five
what did they do for Katie Clive
six seven eight nine ten
gave her a coffin gave her an urn
one two three four five
that's the story of Katie Clive
six seven eight nine ten
she don't need a book
she don't need a pen.

Manoeuvres

While we were beginners
in this war, Teacher knew
all the strategies.
She had the alphabet,
codes, letters, at her command.
All this she protected
by approaching from behind.
Always her element
of surprise – the silent shoes,
a hand that bit
your right shoulder
like a whip to bone.
She'd shake you
like a worthless flag
if things were wrong.
But even so I learnt
some tactics of my own.
I'd play the waiting game,
lie doggo, work slow,
act dumb – less chance
of an error then.
She didn't know, nor did I,
that one day I'd come out
words blazing
years down the line.

Kiss It Better

The cut was gushing
like a gaudy tap
but with my dad there
we'd make it stop.
He'd dab peroxide,
we'd watch it fizz –
so the bandaging began.
On finger, knee or arm
my father worked
winding, binding,
with jaunty spiral folds.
Then he'd bring scissors out,
snip back to form two ends.
Each of them would wrap
around and meet – enough
(I wonder how he knew)
for him to tie a bow
that hugged the hurt or
as he'd say another time,
that fluttered like a butterfly,
a gauzy thing poised
to wing away
with all the pain.

Molly

Here where light slants in to embrace
the sweetsmelling detritus of years
the hens, their neat plush bums upturned,
strut and peck with tawny warbling cries.

The girl has taken Molly for her walk
in the rickety wicker pram
beyond the shifting lace of pepper trees
then out across the run
and through deep red sand.
Now the bird is back in its nest.
The girl at rest on the makeshift perch
might almost be asleep but she is crooning
chook chook chook chook chook
in the chookshed's russet warmth.
She is watching for the chalkwhite egg
she trusts will come. Above them
the iron roof contracts, stretches,
gives grunts of pleasure in the sun.

Nightwatch

That there were wolves about our house
was a secret I knew intuitively.
Never by day but nights you'd sense
a skittering about the place.
Evenings you'd hear their whine
pulsing along the telegraph wires,
a wolfish sound only I recognised.
They'd nose doors then reach higher,
their breath a lesion seen by morning
as a smudge across the windowpane.
Their sway over me was subtle, complete.
From my bed's hot chill I'd lie
waiting, taken by their nearness
shadowed in the blue-black wattle there.

Summer Secrets

Midmorning finds me in the shed,
tools on the bench, the smell of turps . . .
cocooned in the safety of silence.
But not as I think, alone, for something
easing along the border of things
whispers me from the shadow's edge.
A snake is hugging the shed
where wall meets floor, its progress
insistent yet silken as a caress.
Or like a ripple on the riverbank
and that same colour, the colour of mud.
As if following a dream when
my shocked eyes open into night
I watch long after the shape has gone.
But tell no-one, recall not awe nor fear,
only the mystery of movement drawn out,
that warmth in workaday space,
odds and ends crowding a concrete floor,
those wood shavings scattered about.

Seascape

We children would make for the jetty's end,
the sea humping its dark depths,
heaving its fullness dangerously.
Seabirds hung on the seabreeze
jauntily kiting the snappy winds.
Gulls lined the thick white rails.
Nearby, those fishermen
who were our friends.
There was a day when one,
turning almost aside
in haste to retrieve a hook,
with the fish live in his hand
tore, tore, and took away
half the head and the jaw.
We pretended not to see.
The shame wet on our cheeks
we paced to the jetty's end,
stepping out each grained grey plank.
Caught by the wind's teeth there
we cast in vain for words, each separately.

Recollection

Seems everyone can recall
Cliff Nicholson.
Decent bloke, smiling man,
kept the grain store
near the abattoir
and Pluto, the black dog
always sniffing round,
who once found me,
nosed my crotch
through my skimpy dress,
taking in the new
red sweetness there.
My tears, my helpless hands
could not prevail
while his master waited,
watched it all,
waited some more
to savour the scene.
Cliff the decent bloke
then called off his dog,
gave me a wink
and smiled again.

Old Plough

They decided in the end to locate the plough
within the town and on a whim
brought it to earth on the sweep of lawn
beyond the Council Chambers.
There it would have weathered solitary.
But for the memory of the furrow's fall
come generations of sparrows,
light about the wind, about the plough,
the ruffled rows light about the abstract spans
flying open to receive them now,
haphazardly, as in the beginnings.

Compensation

So that, perversely,
he chose always
the best in season –
honey-smelling apricots,
peaches touched with
warm yellow bloom,
a dance of violet grapes,
those plums known by
their opalescent sheen.
Winters, baskets garnished
with bright polished oranges.

Perversely she took them.
'How lovely,' she'd smile.
'What a surprise,' or
'We'll have them tonight.'
He did not accept
those sugary phrases
and year by year
his resentment grew.
Always he'd wait
for a word he knew
she'd never hand over,
a word he coveted –
a straightforward thankyou.

In Grandmother's Garden

Then death and dolls and darkness edged her life,
the maze of portraits in passageways
by night, the dark made strange with tinsel light.
Day smocked the garden with shadows, with flowers,
ribbons of content in the sound of a dove.
Her hours were spent noiselessly.
She, sensual collector of red berries,
lone observer of leaves burning,
the sometime protector of a doll.
The bright sorrow of a pretended grave
would please her, the whiteness of lilies.
Unattended now she roams her garden,
seeks her pattern in pathways,
the perfume of burning leaves
lingering still in a dove's call.

Tribute

Each day, old man slow returning,
he brings to her with his yearning
a single flower – perhaps a rose,
pansy or jasmine, a bit of blossom.
In season a hand of frangipani
pilfered from some garden
he's prized along the way.
This aberrant romance, this act
of simple theft, amuses them.
At night they flirt, beguiled alike
by no bouquet but a vase arranged
by chance. As one they feel
the petals sing, the petals fall,
makeshift spoils unravelling.

At Donovans' Milkbar

Remember the dark lad venturing in?
What was it had happened then?
We took in Mr Donovan's oath,
almost smelt his red fox snarl.
All at once it seemed the shop
spat Black Jack into the street.
The flyscreen door snaps shut, rattles,
shakes in its frame. That noise
puts your heart in your mouth,
sets your teeth on edge,
sends a whiff of fear along the room.
For us some comfort in the lazy fan's
purr. We stir our milkshakes,
sip the sweet milk in, wonder how
it can cool our throats, burn
our foreheads all at the same time.
So we sit there, cat's got our tongues.
We share a grab bag of thoughts,
sense we're on the edge of things.

After The Dance

The evening over, you went your way.

They say that a whole life passes
in front of you when you die
but you reveal no sign of this,
with one hand to your forehead,
a puzzled frown. Yet in an instant
all that is unknown steps out
to partner me, a narrative in black
and white as if on a silent screen.
I take in your perfume, reach for
your sequinned bag, try to gather in
the song of your ballgown spread
flowered across the floor. There
hugging your feet, those sandals
you had always said were tight.

Sanctuary

In the evenings he would wait
high in a duskgold room,
watch, waiting for young lovers
to give flesh to the park below
while a stream of silken memories
whispered, entered him.
As the day seeps away
he surveys the weight of his hands,
opens his mind to the night
down there. Then from his past
comes the smell of crushed leaves,
a dream of yellow hair, bloodfall.

On The River, Late Summer

'Last across the river's a dirty turd,'
he yelled. It was late, it was dark,
they'd had a fair bit
so this time they cheered
when he took to the current,
light as that line he let fly
for cod. And the moon hooked
his freckled white face out there
once twice as he passed by
fast fast in the smudgy night.
They thought they could spot him
until someone said, 'Schultzy's a goner.'
There was silence, the river loud
with his silence as he went down,
headlong downstream to the river bend,
perhaps as far as the ghosted gum
or where the willowed mopoke called.
So when they found him weeks later
he was a soft rolling mass
(his sandshoes still on)
and bait for the box
they'd made ready with holes.
Barry Schultz who'd chat up the girls
(it was rumoured he'd fathered a kid)
who'd round up his mates to paint
the town red. Like they all said
at his send-off, Barry Schultz
had been one hell of a bloke,
good for a laugh, good for a joke.

River Red Gum

The trunk split wide,
edges rolling over
a wound long dried.
Imagine the canoe prised
from this living bark
slipping sleek and silent
away, bodies bent,
arms stitching the boat
to brown water,
the current moving
in one seamless song,
the show of it, the shimmer.

This eucalypt has spanned
life along the river.
Now there's quiet here,
thinking time,
space for a yarn.
You'll catch a crow complain
in the generous branches
above but watch
for vagrant colour,
rosella and lorikeet,
as they flash
larrikin against the green.

On The River

Come summer, the current flowing strong,
the river shimmering, taut between its banks,
we'd row downstream to our picnic ground.
Faster than the shabby paddleboat we skimmed
along, thanks to George whose sinewed hands
dug deep oars into the hurry of water.
Those hot mornings we'd follow the cliff line
where limestone heights sliced the sky.
Down at their base small shaded caves had formed,
secret places with a moss-green smell,
glistening walls awash, the waterweeds entwined
with ferns which surged then fell with the river.

At the bend we bridged the murky current
to the other side. Here great trees welcomed
with arms of shade and enough dead
and fallen branches to last the campfire day.
We children could wander now but not too far,
to stamp on bull ants, gather wood
or help bait and lower yabby traps.
We stopped perhaps to learn how bark canoes
were pulled from birthmarked trunks of gums.
With sausages and chops spitting goodness
to the flames, my mother's basket opened
on a store of salads, sauce and buttered bread,
a soar of cakes and scones, neat lamingtons.
Black-toothed watermelon smiled from a tray.
Time now for my father to make billy tea.
To settle the leaves, one hand outflung,

the other counterbalancing, he twirls
the billy round round on a windmill arm.

Much later we'd make for home again,
cooler, slower, moving upstream. All silent
as we listened to the rhythm of the oars,
a fluid plainsong dripping silver,
or heard the soft plop of a fish out there,
the crown of a whirlpool, halfseen.
Low sun lights on a pelican,
a hover of midges, a dragonfly's blur.
An evening breeze skipping over the river
sends water swirling into the reaches
of my caves where for me still
those ferns mingle, tangle, stir.

KITE LADY

by *Tess Driver*

Tess lives between the sea and the Aldinga
Scrub. Her poetry has featured in the libretto
of the opera 'My Love My Life' and the script
of 'Red'. She has won poetry prizes, most
recently in the South Australian Poetry
Competition. For many years she lived in
England, America and Asia returning to
Australia to teach Communication Skills,
Drama, English and Creative Writing.
Completing an M.A at Adelaide University,
she now writes full time.

ACKNOWLEDGMENTS

'Flying on a Persian Carpet' written for RED,
produced by Pat Rix for Vitalstatistix; 'Ritual'
written for RED produced by Pat Rix for
Vitalstatistix; 'This Afternoon I Fly To Paris'
prize 2001 SA Poetry Festival, Fleurieu
Peninsula.

THE POEMS

Sea

Baited   34
Through A Mist   35
Whispered Desire   36
Stones For Breakfast   37
After September 11th 2001   38
Grey Dawn   39
Kissing Music   40
The Bite   41
Burning Whispers   42

Land

Moving Poems I, II, III   43
Let The Sunshine In   47
Ritual   48
Summer   49
Flying On A Persian Rug   50
Dance The Villano   51
Yellow Roses   52

People

Alice In Wonderland   53
The Shed   54
Kite Lady   55
Apple Pie   56
Window Gazer   57
Hurt   58
This Afternoon I Fly To Paris   59

Baited

Fishing boats,
full stops anchoring.
The end of the line
for baited things,
hidden deep
like thoughts.

Through A Mist

Rain drifts like thought
across the window.

I watch him bend and pull,
that lone oarsman, rowing out to sea
on a cold day.

He is shrouded now in mist,
thick across the water,
no line between sea and sky.

Too tired to be honest,
too afraid to be alone,
too lost in fog to look inside,

I'm looking now.

It hurts.

Whispered Desire

One hundred ibis fly like whispers
across blue.
Sun, ripe as mango flesh
sinks into a stern horizon.
Erotic thoughts ripple across water,
dive deep under rosy sea,
surface into blushing dusk.

Stones For Breakfast

Morning creeps, heavy as a yawn.
Smoke slides up chimneys,
radios thunder.
      Civil wars mean children keep on starving.
      In another grisly corner of the world,
      a severed head is bartered for F16s.
Stones rattle like bones of history
beneath the incoming tide.

After September 11th 2001

The last bird flies
heavy across the sea.
I cut geranium heads at dusk,
listen as tireless talk-back
replays September screams,
drowns old certainties
and security of place.
No blinding sunset tonight,
the truth is too painful
for technicolour skies
and rainbow sea.
The surfer, skin chilled
turns with sighs of tide,
to ride to shore
no promises in uncertain times.
Snip the last geranium head
as darkness falls.

Grey Dawn

A kestrel hovers, dives, a bullet on its kill.
Grey parchment cliffs
giant feet, gnarled toes
clutch at the sea of waves,
purple taffeta of a wild waltz.

Wind howls at dawn
through rye grass paddocks.
Cockies' claws scrape
and clatter on the roof.

Fishermen cough, stop cleaning their rods,
thump inside for cups of tea.
No boats will launch today.

Kissing Music

Wind carries strokes of violins
across the dunes,
languorous echoes that shimmer
over grey grass.
Bach's strings in G
like kisses ripple
amongst the waves forever,
stroking, stroking the shore.

The Bite

On the roof
parrots scrape and shuffle
screech like market-stall spruikers
fling early morning gossip into cold air
cars yawn in the pink dawn
fishermen in boats in an oyster sea
fling hooked and baited lines
then watch them sink into the deep
searching for that last desperate dream
before day bites.

Burning Whispers

Sea simmers,
stream of consciousness weather.
Dogs gasp,
kids flop like fish out of water
scaly with sun.

A chestnut horse, glinting bronze,
flounders like a wet dream
in the sea, still as a pond.
Such cool lapping
like burning whispers,
an opening line of creeping foam,
endless introduction to a mystery.

Moving Poems

I

Where the cedar bed sat
4 dents in the carpet
undisturbed for thirty years.
Packed in pieces
like dreams
when one wakes up too soon.

The dressing table,
emptied of the underwear,
the jewels, the scarves, the bags,
accessories to adorn
the mirror's image that
cannot smile today.

II

The dog knows.
She sniffs the corners
where dead spiders, fluff
have crouched for years
behind the wardrobe.

The clothes have gone,
each season packed in bags.
Coat hangers swing,
weightless in the dark
where mothballs roll.

A two door, corpseless coffin,
loaded on a trolley
by sweating men in red.

III

Leaves on afternoon gums,
heat yellowed,
drop and skate
on hard brown earth.

I water my garden,
the last time.
Skinks race silver grey,
skippering on brittle twigs.
Monarch butterflies
frantic as my thoughts,
alight then flit, alight then flit
on ferns,
hydrangea,
iris,
lavender,
rose.

I remember planting
all of them,
crowbarred olives, cotton bush,
until my body screamed, 'no more'.

I watched a paper plan
become French windows,
stuccoed walls,
leadlight full of curves
that blushed at naked bodies
and glowed around the sleeping child.
The cedar table, scratched and polished,
mirroring laughter
spilling deep into the night.

And winter fog,
black branches silhouetted,
stripped of all the might have beens.

Around the hearth,
conversation hangs on the walls,
mulled and rich
as vintaged years,
prized paintings
that need no frames.

Let The Sunshine In

White moon,
a dead fish's eye, in the sky,
in the middle of the day.

Dogs howl,
dance their frenzy along the fence.
Two crows,
black and loud,
fill the sky with menace.

Cyclops' blind eye
scans the land below,
gorging on the vanities
and griefs released
when Odysseus let the sun
into his cave.

Ritual

Seeds, a fecund sign.
They fall from pods when split
to fill the plate for ritual feasts.
A willow-patterned bowl
with birds of blue.
They eat the seeds
then spill them wide to fertilize
an ancient soil
where pomegranates grow.
Their luscious pulp and seeds
are spooned by lovers
to each other's lips.
The ritual of food repeats, repeats
and round and round
the cycle will begin again.
An endless circle,
life within a pea
or pomegranate
in its ruddy skin.

Summer

Brazen gums
fling cracking bark
into the heat.
White smooth limbs
stripped bare
for the sun's caress.

Moonlight serenades.
Leaves shiver in the glow.
Dumb to the seduction,
koalas munch.

Flying On A Persian Rug

Flushed strawberries flirt
with chillies
on a Persian rug.

A white-flowered plant
bearing juicy, red fruit,
cannot copulate
with chillies . . .
red, acrid, pungent,
used for stews with beef.

The only thing in common
is the colour of their skin,
red.

And all the magic
of mysterious runes
will not sweeten
this incompatibility.

Dance The Villano

Dark as the beauty of a lace mantilla.
Guitar and voices soar in Spanish song
of discant melody.

History whips beneath the score.
Spaniards hacking Indians
in bloody lust.

I hear the screams
amongst the rising cadence
of glorious sound.

Hopi Indian women,
the peaceful people,
moan for tortured warriors.

Tears fall
and turn to black obsidian.
I hold them in my hand

Black, shiny stones,
cold and smooth,
a legend of grief.

Yellow Roses

Philip Glass splits shards over bitumen
disturbs the confident roll of tyres
clouds the highway horizon
disintegrates white lines
shatters determined destinations.

The rear view mirror frames the cross
bearing yellow roses
at the side of the road.

She was sixteen when she hit
the concrete stobie pole.

Alice In Wonderland

Alice is a wraith
dancing in the sea.
A large, pale moon
embroiders waves as
Alice dips and glides,
a skimmering creature.
She wraps her body
in a seaweed shawl,
seashells jangle in the dark
garlanding soft skin.
On land her smile is bright and taut.
The string soars high,
but kites are never free.
The monsters of the day hold tight
and bring them down to earth.
Darkness and the sea and moon
hide ugly things
with smudgy glow.
Alice flies at night
until the chorused birds of dawn
light the net of day.

The Shed

He walks with bandy legs
to the temple down the back
lured by grease and oil,
incense of a communion
closed to detergent minds.
The spanners, wrenches,
hammers, nuts and bolts are
not for hands which use domestic tools.
No baking mind that's vacuumed clean
could ever know the joy he feels.
She calls it "dirt", but it is his!
He spends the precious hours with friends
in anxious motor talk
around a beer
beneath a calendar which shows pneumatic blondes.
A private place
where robes are overalls
and no one shrills, "Take off your boots!"

Kite Lady

Kite lady stretches, runs fingers
through stringy, grey hair.
It's windy today on the beach,
good for selling kites . . .
there's a surf life-saving carnival.

Once it was her beach.
Every Sunday, she and Bill
dragged old bags of meat,
pulled the worms, long as snakes
from the sand
as the tide sucked out.

Fishermen bought them for a dollar.
But the government put a tax on worms
and Bill died.

Kites are prettier than worms
and no smell of rancid meat
in the beat-up station-wagon,
just strings and plastic and colour.
Red, orange, blue, green, yellow
fill the beach with weekend rainbows.

If only she could fly.

Apple Pie

The dog moans in the kennel.
She turns the car onto asphalt,
grinding gears, sweat on the steering wheel,
dog hair on the seat.

She listens,
still hears his dog.
Closes the window, tight,
now only silence.

She drives wildly,
remembers apples, fallen apples,
picked up in Autumn.

They walked in the orchard,
wicker basket dangling,
fingers touching,
silent together,
shoes scrunching on dry earth.

She will buy apples,
make his favourite pie.
Cinnamon, cloves, shortcrust pastry,
she will eat it all with cream,
watch T.V. very late
and eat potato chips and chocolate in bed.

No-one there
to make her feel guilty.

Window Gazer

Suburban flab has no place here.
Gym trim, they strut
the bitumen catwalk,
plate glass smiles reflect
narcissistic display.

The café set,
shadowed in the latté steam,
talk of my and me and my,
camouflaged success
in the filtered cigarette,
scarred by shrill lipstick laughs.

Two cappuccinos,
made with skimmer milk,
balance on a table
on the pavement.

Madonna holds a baby to her breast.
Business men, munching dried tomato,
goat cheese lunch on rye,
avert their gaze.
An apricot poodle lifts its leg.

Hurt

Her helmet hair was smooth
shiny as a lie.
He said goodbye,
the only word spoken
as they parted,
two children between their bristling dislike.

Shirt unironed,
hair scrunched in angry curls,
he held the baby close.

Called the other,
the little girl,
blonde and small
rigid and still
as a courier parcel.

The mother
turned and stomped away
neat pleats swishing
the past.

Neither child cried.

This Afternoon I Fly To Paris

Salt damp and aphids
a garden full of weeds
dead flowers in a vase.

Dirty football shorts
dog hairs on the sofa
no petrol in the car
no milk left in the fridge
red broken fingernail
rust marks in the bath.

I am in Albert Hall playing harpsichord
with Musica Antiqua
my hair is long and red
my skin is milky soft
the audience cries "encore, encore!"

Life gets in the way.

Today I am Matilda, concert queen,
yesterday, Genevieve of culinary fame,
last week, Teresa, star of stage and film.

In May I dived in Greece,
drank Bolinger and ate Beluga caviar
sent by a fishing magnate
fascinated by my charm.

Hang the washing out,
collect the kids from school
grill the chops and sausages
iron the shirts with starch.

I am sailing up the Amazon
searching for a friend who's lost in Rio.
I visit Gabriel Garcia Marquez
who likes my work.
We drink tequila in a bar
and talk of Hemingway and Junot Diaz.

Now it's Friday,
time for cleaning floors
supermarket shopping
going to the bank for cash.

This afternoon
            I
         fly
            to
               Paris.

FINE RAIN STRAIGHT DOWN

by *David Mortimer*

David Mortimer wrote a lot of poems up to
the age of twenty, then very few for two
decades. In the last five years he has found
himself writing extensively and happily on a
range of issues and interests. His poems are
written to be read out loud or heard in the
mind – to be enjoyed as sound and rhythm as
well as argument and idea.

ACKNOWLEDGEMENTS

'Granny Smiths In A Bowl' previously published in *Friendly Street Reader 26* (2002); 'Outer Harbour Line' previously published in *TransAdelaide Express* (November 2000); 'Wharf Market' previously published in the *Adelaide Review* (July 2000) and *Friendly Street Reader 25* (2001). 'Wharf Market', 'Onions' and 'Port Adelaide' broadcast on 5UV Radio Adelaide 101.5 fm *Writers Radio* (October 2002); thank you to Angela McKenzie for reading and to Jim Mortimer for the recording. Thank you to Josie Mortimer for the photograph, to all my family and friends, to Friendly Street, and to Jan Owen for her perceptive comments on this collection and its title.

For Angey, Cate, Jon and Will

THE POEMS

Week-End	64
Singularity	65
Bed	66
Callistemon	67
Expectation	68
In S.A.N.F.L., Even A.F.L.	69
Music	70
Eyes	71
Morality	72
This Year's Children	73
Granny Smiths In A Bowl	74
Nameless	75
Sometimes	76
Natural Selection	76
The Whirlwind	77
Dad	78
Bird-Watching	79
Continuum	80
Outer Harbour Line	80
Wharf Market	81
Onions	82
Port Adelaide	83
Sufi Music Comes On The Radio	84
T.V. Cooks	85
Maths/Science	86
Fine Rain Straight Down	86
Asylum	87
"Flying Planes Can Be Dangerous"	88
Adelaide Suburban	89
The Given	90

Week-End

Saturday morning quietness
The cat miaowing/ against the screen
A few birds/ unhurriedly/ syrup the air
The Bottlebrush/ still as a curtain/ While
Across the lawn/ at every soundless step
A million souls' suburban not not sleep
Is caught/ and held/ disturbed/ relieved/ returned
To breathing/ breathing-out
To a breathing out of bruises

Singularity

Causation is nowhere if
All the world is one event
Spring of a butterfly's wing stiff
With no meaning in the cyclone's course
And billiard-balls and planets sent
At angles skewed like letters in a name
Told like whimsies in a story
That accumulate but lay no claim
To deeper plays of force on force
Or formulae for simpler glory
More than the one continual unfolding
Awkward shape that always was
Already-all-of space and time and holding
Everywhere at bay the word – because

Bed

I pursue you up a corridor of bed
Or more like a Giotto fresco
Narrow like the inside of a score-board
Ladders and stairs and Ptolemaic wheels
And barely room to slide our halos past

In an almost-flat world without gravity
Where weightless touches each describe a spin
A somersault the angels watch
Direct through clouds roof ceiling sheets
The hand-held wide-screened liquid-crystal display

Is pressed so that eddies carry us around
And round and round imagined corners kept
In a fast slow stop start pulse
Beyond the exercise of will or friction traction
Where in each direction parallels intersect

Callistemon

Awfully tall and
Teetering with birds
Our bottle-brush has grown

Supplely taller again
By lengths that do not look green
But are

And will be
Next year's hard wood;

How can it
Surely tallest
Slowly keep upping

Year by year

While all its
Arcing strings and
Swinging leaves and
Tufted lures
Dissemble downwards?

Expectation

Forty thousand years of rain
Ratchetting out of the sky
Each and every now and again
And then a year like this, dry

As an inductive argument
Creeks and buckets, gutters, yards
Begging a conclusion sent
From any god *ex machina*, guards

Against pretence to know or hide
The still quiet panic of reason
That the sun will rise tomorrow, stars slide
To appointed places, days into season

In S.A.N.F.L., Even A.F.L.

Some people who play
From the first springs of joy, of love
Of game of speed for speed's
Sake sheer anticipation cleverness
Like a cat/ a bird/ a leaping ant's
Flight/ in your eye/ breath-
Taking conversion of pace in space
To height

Grip
Imagination, but

May still apply, may even find a place
In club, in league,
Before the coaches, commentators and
The carping fans can do-their-worst (with word on word)
    to chase
The warm anatomy of this
Or that mistake/ away
(To drill defence within attack instil disgrace)

But even through this grim
Experience
A quickly moving whim, a wilful strength, a wild
    exuberance danced
And chanced to the highest level
Is not unheard

Music

That physiology should flower at a sound
Of voices bled together stand astonished:
Why should the ear be bent to so be drawn?
And why the skin to fingers' drum be driven?
Couldn't this tent of conscious life been pegged
Without a risk that stretching pattern poised
From point to point would waken worlds in worlds
Which swoop and rush harass on whispered wings?

This teleology requires a richer pause
Than evolutionists can shrug a pretty pose
Mumbling emergent properties while keeping clear
Of explanation or prediction that a clock could counter
So eagerly creationists preach doubt
From labelled bottles as a daily draught
That patient priests decant despair
In crystal cut for drinking dearer
Mysteries more serious than faith or science:
Monotonous miracles of constant sequence.

Eyes

As if from through
The
Window of a car
You
Have found a way to look
Back
While steering at the new
View

And so your eyes
Kill
More suddenly behind
Than
Metal Engine Glass
Thrust
Fast into a man
Can

Morality

Early morning watering
Standing with the hose
Laying up treasure in earth

Readying plants
Like with a good breakfast
For the day's moiling heat

Steadying stems
And leaves to stomach
A warfare of light to come

And doing it right
(Not like those who -
Reckless of snails – watered last night)

(And never as these
Caught mid-afternoon spraying
Dust and sun and a hot breeze)

This Year's Children

Everywhere wildness appears – in pushers,
Parks and playgrounds –
Rage and tears –
But more so in the bright, tight,
Frightening openness of smiles –
The sure pursuit of every appetite

(Bemoaning the loss of wilderness,
We fail to see – it rising past our ears
And through our blood)

And if we think the years –
The socializing years, anaesthetising,
Boredom, the parade of fears –
Make one sip of difference
To these sober souls' intensity of strangeness
We're mad . . . or thick as mud

Granny Smiths In A Bowl

Apples not of earth but of
Some green and grievous sea
That tangles the tops of branches
Worrying buds to flower, flowers to orb

Catching the eyes, the hands
Of a recklessly under-aged diver

Carried in, heaped on the half-shell
Dazzling the room with their reflective sheen

While the casually caught-up leaves
Speak a week of losing moisture gracefully
Curling toward sea-weed or silk
Retirement

These pomme-de-non-terre glow
To a different ethic inward and outward
Readiness rough-smooth ripeness
And if rubbed against the teeth the promise
Rich

Nameless

Sea-bird
On the jetty
Taking no nonsense
From the likes of us

Beautiful brown
Wing-span
And a slow strength

Curved above water
Then coming to rest

Curved above water
Then coming to rest

Spends me, sends me, spilling
Half the sun-shrunk afternoon
Turned and culled across
Electronic petals, looking
For a name to handle

All this useless,
Curious, madness

Sometimes

Sometimes one comes some
Times another
Glitter of pleasure

And the deep hook
Blubbered and hung

Shivers more

Than pound on pound
On pound of salty green
And arcing wind can tug

Natural Selection

The poets everywhere
Continue to sing
The landscape into life

Places everywhere
Create their own curators

Beyond death
The wilder the better
Stories grip the earth

The Whirlwind

Tougher than history
More, much more than
Even O'Reilly warned was sown

The hard reality
Wilder and wider spun
Than imagination's whirlwind blown

Leg-spin reborn
Pitches not even worn
By wrist-wrung mischief torn

And what shoulder
And what art could
Twist the windows of the dawn

After all the years
The tedious speed creed
Stamped down earth with murderous glance

The ball now hauls
The back foot forward
Hands, heart, mind teach dust to dance

Dad

You told me, although I didn't need
The extra layer of meaning, how the peace descended

Suddenly, in the same exhausted
Grasp of night when no phone rang

You knew your wife had died

Certainly, as if she'd said good-bye

You felt the release, the gone-from-earth
Relief, touch, before the huge, the tidal

Wave of grief you woke us to had tumbled
Morning and everything up-side-drowned

Years before we found our feet again

Bird-Watching

Despite the slash/ Of beak and claw,
The razor in the grim dove's breast,
And bickered feathers on the floor
Of well-kept parks/ we find a rest—
Better than all our knowledge weaves—
In watching birds with ceaseless pump
Of heart and wings along the sleeves
And cuffs of air plunge pulse and jump

Against an always side-ways wider sphere
Of choice between the buildings and the trees
A thousand paths an hour swung deft and clear
Dividing space and time by new degrees
Mirror the spirits that the sweet notes steer
Into a sky of song/ With forceful ease

Continuum

Hurried into clothes
I carry your perfume on me, on my skin
Shallower
Than any chafing won't release, ling-
-ering our purpose on the wide day's dutiful quadrille
Movement by movement, moment by moment
Knowing the nub of the compass hinged above
Follows and holds, re-animating
Each thought flown to the warmth
Of this our stickier commerce

Outer Harbour Line

Thirty degrees from the eastern earth
The sun begins its work of warmth
We board a train, and settle to books
Newspapers, magazines, conversations

The powerless and those not yet
Inducted to their power share
The crystal sunlight strained through glass
Slow-hauled from shade to flickering dazzle

Above behind between the trees
Houses and stobie poles, streets and wires
Still in a crust of night untouched
Magritte-shaped stories of absence and presence

Wharf Market

Chop the workers up for berley
See what sharks come in
To eat the poor

See! See! The sharks! What fine
Efficient teeth they have!
What bite! What jaw!

Quickly attract them fast and early
They'll hang around for more
See how they grin

They'll advertise the blood through brine
Compete to gnaw and shave
The bone the skin

Onions

How many onions, eased from earth,
And bundled, bagged and bound around Australia
In iridescent orange plastic netting tightly glozed
Ten kilo scrotal sacks
Slung onto concrete fruit-shop floors
Or stacked along supermarket benches
Humbly wait the choice, the knife, the service
Ready, in their calling, finally, to satisfy
Even our monumental lust for chutney?

Port Adelaide

Seagull scrambles through a mid-morn sky
Squawking the taste of salt
The shoppers buy
Slow in their padding from soft tyred cars
To the auto-telling vault
And chocolate bars

A wider sense of calmness rising here
The current-worried cost
Can disappear
Deeper than old disputes have flared
Or ships been lost
Or camp-fires shared

Beyond before the scratches of the hands
On sticks or stones
The constant land's
Market with a river and a tide
Exchange of sand for bones
For shells supplied

Sufi Music Comes On The Radio

Splendidly serious, they place the feet religiously
Inside the memory, in the market square, on the T.V.
Light step soft the shoed feet in the barely-awake
Before-the-cricket dozing darkness

And then I guessed, but now
I know them now, can name them
Dervishes not like we were warned
When we were whirling
Red couch cordialled
Out-of-control children

These were precise, and are
And outside control, beyond precision
Inside the very essence of why anybody ever bothered
Dance, or even to move, to move at all

Each step a division

T.V. Cooks

Kind how they come
On every channel
Just before the program that you want
Or in the middle
Of rolling numbers on an advert break

Full of technique
They cut and crush, they brush with oil
Boil and baste and bake and peel
Reserve the stock, remove the core
And chop and chop and chop and chop
And speak and speak and speak and speak
And speak and speak and speak

Maths/Science

Death. Death.
Whoever needed that breath?
The chemistry goes on
And on and on and on and
Into chemical infinity

The theory
Inside every heart-hole
Worming further

Plus one, plus one, plus one

The shovels disinter eternity

Fine Rain Straight Down

Between wet and dry
You learn to live
Watching puddles and drips and rainbows
And Rothko oblongs under cars

The way trees are not umbrellas
And leaves and branches sieve
Ever after clouds stop

Grey and blue and green and black
Take and give

Asylum

What do we exactly fear?
The touch of foot on land?
The thump of boat against the pier?

Darker than we can understand
Why screaming wings and tyres on tarmac
Don't threaten like the quiet sea

To make us want to push them back
And turn away and shut our eyes and be
Ready to legislate our blindness

We fear the human face and the message sent
From us and to us of our own kindness

And that's no compliment

"Flying Planes Can Be Dangerous"

Flying planes can be dangerous
How quickly have people assimilated this idea
The deep structure forever changed
The syntax of the skies now clear
In ways we'd never thought to parse
The old two-headed truism
In just the same words, with the same sound
    and meaning
But a wholly-renovated fear

Adelaide Suburban

It's that soft time of almost night
Roses burn along the street
Just with the clarity of their own wattage
And everything is lit with its own wattage

In a kind of equilibrium
That we want to call the true, the real
The actual colour of each colour
Speaking to us without coercion of light or dark

And so that even shadows give up secrets
Give up being shadows in a way
Unthinkable at any other time
To eyes that merely wander in

The Given

Our gifts are given over and again
Not lost not hidden but shining
Through each thing we do each
Morning the same begins our work and every
Night our dreaming resumes a
Remembering of Light our life
Of dark our death our speech it
Sings/ takes wing/ takes wing/ and draws and drives
One word from end to end from
Earth to earth; and through
The secret waters of the ground
The roots derive a fuel
We cannot help but burn
And give and give and give and give